Think Up And Go Up!

There is POWER in positive thinking!

ANDREA FREEMAN

Copyright ©2013 Andrea Freeman

All Rights Reserved. No part of this book may be reproduced or transmitted in any form or by any means, electronic or mechanical, including photocopying, recording, or by any information storage and retrieval system, without prior written permission from the Author/Publisher of this book, except for the inclusion of brief quotations in printed reviews.

Scripture taken from New Century Version Bible

ISBN: 978-0-615-89081-4 Published in U.S. by Changing Lives And Sincerely Supporting You, Inc. ⍰

Contents

Thanks To God Prayer..4

A Note From The Author..6

Authors Prayer For Readers......................................7

Chapter 1: What Influences Your Thinking?.....8

Chapter 2: Evaluate Your Circle Of Influence..19

Chapter 3: Work Smart...26

Chapter 4: How Can You Benefit Others?......35

Chapter 5: How To Attract The Right People..45

REFLECT: Experiences During Reading...........53

Chapter 6: Become An Expert............................59

Chapter 7: Challenge Yourself............................66

Chapter 8: Take Action...73

Chapter 9: Be Determined To Win....................81

Chapter 10: From Motivation To Elevation.....87

REFLECT: Experiences During Reading...........94

Inspirational Quotes...98

Contact The Author..106

Thanks To God Prayer

Father, I come to You in the Name of Jesus, my Lord and my Savior. I come to You with a heart of thanksgiving. I thank You for all the good things in my life, for You are the Creator of all things good. Father, I thank You for Your Presence, for in Your Presence is the fullness of my joy and in Your Presence I am complete and whole. In Your Presence I have purpose. Because of Your Presence, I am glad to be here. Father, I thank You for Your plan, that I might have a full life with joy and have it in abundance to overflowing. Father, I thank You for Your provision, that all my needs are met according to Your riches in glory and that I may prosper in all areas of my life as my soul shall prosper. Father, I thank You for Your protection, that Your perfect love casteth out all fear and that no weapon formed against me shall prosper. Father, I thank You for Your peace. The peace that passes all understanding. The peace that keeps me calm and secure through adversity. The peace that leads me through all the storms that come into my life. Father, thank You for my life and Your Presence in it. In the mighty name of Jesus, Amen.

A Note From The Author

Greetings Friends, in the name of the Lord. I am extremely grateful to have an opportunity to share with you how to "Think Up And Go Up" so that you may move forward, and be elevated to the next level in your life. God Bless You!

Authors Prayer For Readers

Heavenly Father, I call on you to cast down any feelings of fear, doubt, or failure. I ask that any restrictions on their lives be removed by removing the barriers that have held them captive. Father God, I ask that you will increase and strengthen their faith, and I pray that they will come into divine alignment. I decree and declare that this book will change the course of their destiny and that their lives will be blessed beyond measure. In the mighty name of Jesus I pray, AMEN!

1 *What Influences Your Thinking?*

Do you know that our perception or how we perceive things is what primarily affects our thinking? Another words, the attitudes that we developed based on an impression or understanding of what we observed or thought highly affects the way we think. We perceive things through our sense of sight, smell, taste, hearing, and touch. At the end of the day, what we think will definitely influence what we do. However, becoming aware of our influences will make it much easier to accept and implement a plan to having a positive attitude.

Two major influences to a person's thinking are:

Family

Your family is often the strongest positive or negative influence in your life. Growing up and being raised with your family can either be an asset or a road block to the way you learn how to feel, think and act in society. Although our beliefs, views, morals, and values can be decided by ourselves, they are characterized by our families.

As young children, we cannot choose how we live, our parents do. They teach and show us what they have learned. They are the ones that we share our opinions with, watch, and pay attention to as we grow in life. Therefore, they have a lot of influence in our lives. Often parent's don't realize that they are teaching their children things that they don't intend to because, "more things are caught than taught."

On the other hand, families are the most important part of a human's life but as you grow older, you can start to make your own choices. The older you grow, the less influence they have on your life. As people mature, they are often seeking other role models that they consider to be professional, or successful. For example: Stars are considered role models or people to look up to.

Friends

Friends are also a huge influence in your life. Friendships can encourage you to live and be the best you can be, boost your self-esteem, or even help enhance the quality of your life. They are built over time, within months and sometimes even years. Friends are very important to you. They are often the ones you trust the most. They are your sounding boards and mirrors. During the time in which you are building a friendship, you get to a point where you begin to feel comfortable being there for one another.

You often go to friends and share your joys and problems because, you look to them to express their feelings and give advice. On the other hand, friends can be mentally or physically exhausting , draining, and negative. Separating from those friends can be difficult because of the comfort level they have with you, and changing that would not benefit them. It has been said, "show me your friends, and I will show you your future."

Other influence's to a person's thinking are:

<u>Environment</u>

What is your home, social, and work environment like?

Career

What type of career do you have? Do you enjoy it? Is it stressful?

Health

How would you rate your health? Good, average, or poor and why?

Past Experiences

What are some experiences that you had which affected your life, whether it's positive or negative?

Circumstances

What are your current circumstances and how do they make you feel?

Reading

What types of literature do you read and how are you learning from it? How does it contribute to your personal or professional growth?

Listening

What are you listening to (music, people, etc.)? How does it affect your daily life?

Watching

What do you watch (television, movies, public, etc.) and what are you learning from it?

Personal Choices

What type of personal choices have you made over the past year and how have they benefited you?

Self-Esteem

How do you perceive yourself and what type of self-talk do you have?

Now that you have an idea of what influences your thinking, it's up to you to decide or choose what you will or will not allow to influence you in a negative manner. Let me talk a little about relationships and associations.

Of course you cannot choose who you are related to but, you can choose how you associate with them. Whether the people you associate with are positive or negative, it's only a matter of time before you are the same way. If they are negative, and you seemed to think that some of the things they did were unthinkable, you will eventually gain a new perspective and those things will become the norm. You slowly but surely reflect the behavior of them.

Sometimes you feel let down by friends, and lessons may be "painful but necessary" to your inner growth. You must not tolerate mediocrity from others, because you will begin to find mediocrity acceptable in your own life as well. You must change this. Yes, it will be hard but it's better to be alone than to be in the wrong company.

Start taking a little inventory of the people you are associated with and ask yourself, what qualities have you adopted from each of them? How have they influenced your attitudes, confidence, character traits, self-esteem, and your acceptance of yourself?

Recognize that the ones who are slowly but surely pulling you down, "DON'T WANT YOU TO GROW." For the result of your personal growth, will be outgrowing them in their comfort zone. Not that they are jealous of you, but they feel the need to keep you on the same level of relating to their negativity and they fear losing that. GET RID OF THEM! Start scratching negative people off of the list, until the list only consists of the names of people who add value to your life.

You must also practice being conscious of your reactions and realities. Sometimes we over react about small things. We allow some of the least important things to affect how we feel and think. Some situations and circumstances are so temporary, but we often create a lifetime of grief over them. Many people are still blaming their childhood for their adult choices and challenges.

They are often harboring resentment or attachment to the past, and we have developed attitudes which are negative and full of doubt. You must have an attitude of gratitude, because you will never see what your future holds if you can't stop looking back at your past.

    Neuroscientists have written that the adult brain and personality are not "set" but rather, continue to grow and mature based on new ideas, experiences, and conditioning. Are you conditioning your mind to believe that you will live the life of your dreams? Are you thinking of at least ONE idea that you will take massive action on? Be optimistic about the future and that optimism will work like a magnet, drawing that desired future to you.

<u>Chapter Checkpoint:</u>

What has influenced the way you think?

Have other people been able to influence you with their way of thinking? If so, why?

What is it that you find negatively controls your thinking and why?

What will you do to change your negative influences?

What will you do to make sure that you are being a positive influence to everyone you interact with?

How has your thinking changed since you read this chapter?

2 *Evaluate Your Circle Of Influence*

The people you spend the most time with are primary factors in how successful you will be in life. Motivational speaker Jim Rohn says, "You are the average of the five people you spend the most time with." That is relating to their lifestyles, manners, incomes, etc. If you don't believe it, visit a prison and ask any inmate what kind of friends they had prior to their conviction.

Being connected to the right people will not only keep you away from trouble, but also helps you to fight your way through hardships. It can help you reach high levels of success. That is why it is of utmost importance to carefully select the people you will associate with.

Successful people are very focused on what they want to be doing. Their week and weekend look very similar; always focusing on creating the life they truly desire to live. Successful people always participate in creative activities and connect with creative people, to consistently exercise their brain.

Constantly creating and being relevant to their work, is a secret weapon in professional success. Therefore, they usually achieve a measure of happiness and fulfillment in their work, family, and spiritual life.

Chapter Checkpoint:

Who are the 5 (3 minimum) people in your life that you spend the most time with?

What do they do with their lives?

How ambitious are they?

How happy, optimistic, and enthusiastic are they?

How successful have they been?

Due to the need of feeling a sense of accomplishment, most successful people are self-motivated and ready to face the next challenge in life. They are always reflecting, processing, and thinking of the bigger issues.

Be sure to stay surrounded by people with shared interests, who can help spark ideas about what you are passionate about. Establish and cultivate relationships with people of professional organizations, volunteer groups, fundraising events, and the local community to add to your life balance.

How distinct you are and how you stay connected with your peers is vitally important to your positioning. Networking shouldn't be an event, it should be a lifestyle. That way, you begin to stand out, attract better people, and create a brand that your peers want to be a part of and promote. It's a very tough world, that's why it is critical that you are connected to smart professionals who help sharpen your mind and better equip you for success.

If you want to be wealthy, spend time with wealthy people. Stop making yourself believe that you must already be wealthy to hang around them. Highly successful people hang around people who are already performing at the level at which they want to perform. They are not hanging around and expecting to learn from people who are moving in a backward or negative direction, or only earn 50% of what they currently earn. Book signings, business breakfast's, lunch and learn events, club membership, and leadership events are great places to hangout and meet wealthy people; NOT CLUBS AND BARS!

Chapter Checkpoint:

Who and how has anyone contributed to your real joy and passion for your work?

Who have you connected with over the past 6 months that have helped you achieve or exceed financial milestones? How did they help?

What will you do to make sure that you are connected with the right people?

If surrounding yourself with the right people means losing some family and friends, "DON'T BE AFRAID TO LOSE." Instead of becoming the average of some average people, DIP WITH THE BEST! Find people who are focused, determined, enthusiastic, and dying to be incredibly successful, happy, and doing whatever it takes to chase their dreams. When you find them, CLING TO THEM! Try learning as much as you can from their skill set, to get you lifted onto the NEXT LEVEL.

Being encouraged to connect with the right people, and to disconnect from the wrong people, is not meant to try and convince you to dislike certain people. The bible says, "Don't make friends with quick-tempered people or spend time with those who have bad tempers. If you do, you will be like them. Then you will be in real danger." Proverbs 22:24-25 (NCV) Take a hard look at your circle of influence. Is it time to expand or grow it, or is it time to change it?

3 *Work Smart*

Have you ever wished that you could find a way to work smarter instead of harder? Have you ever felt as if there aren't enough hours in a day to accomplish your tasks? Well, there are really enough hours in a day for you to accomplish whatever you wish. You may have to spend a little more time rearranging and managing your time more wisely, but you can be very productive.

Some people think that if they are working more or longer hours, they are working smarter. The key to working smarter is not to work extra hours, but to get the best results in less time. In order for that to happen, you must change how you work. You must ask yourself what things can be done more efficiently or eliminated altogether.

Many people are working but aren't actually getting any work done. Whether we like it or not, work has become a lifestyle and it has become increasingly inefficient. Studies actually show that 60% or less of work time is actually spent productively, due to constant distractions that often cause productivity to take a back seat.

Chapter Checkpoint:

On an average day, how many tasks do you intend to complete within an eight hour time frame?

How often do you successfully complete all of your daily tasks within the desired time frame?

How do you feel about multi-tasking?

What do you do to make sure that you are remaining focused and staying on task?

What are some of your major distractions?

If you really desire to work smarter, STOP WASTING TIME! You must consider working more strategically and get into a zone, like you are running a marathon. In order to do so, you must learn how to effectively "manage your time" by first eliminating all of your major distractions.

Eliminating your distractions will help you zoom in and bring full focus to ONE task, while building momentum until you begin to produce unlimited results. Being productive enables a higher quality of life.

Some of our major distractions are email, cell/telephone, meetings, and YOURSELF. Let me share with you how these distractions become your biggest time wasters.

Email

You receive so many e-mails, that it's easy to spend at least two hours of your eight hour work day reading, and replying to them. That ends up being 25 percent of your time and in most cases it doesn't produce at least 25 percent of your income. Although it's one of the simplest and easiest ways to make contact, you spend much of your time going through unavoidably and pointless emails. Most people check their emails over and over throughout each day, and it takes at least 15 minutes to refocus after each time. You spend hours just trying to manage it. It's a low value added activity.

Cell/Telephone

You spend time checking cell and telephone messages and returning calls. Often, the calls are extended by having small talk conversation, that is totally unrelated to the primary reason for the call. After clearing out all of your messages, returning all of your calls, and beginning to focus on getting some work done, the phone begins to ring again. It not only takes you out of your flow but gets you side tracked onto something else. At the end of it all, you struggle to refocus on what you must complete.

Meetings

You plan meetings that are often huge time wasters. Some people think that meeting face to face is the most effective way to make progress. In many cases, they are unproductive because they are not planned out very well. There is no clear agenda, and oftentimes too many people are having discussions that don't always pertain to their specific responsibilities. This makes it difficult to reach decisions during the time allotted for the meeting.

Yourself

So often, your biggest distractions will come from yourself. Many times you are trying to multi-task, thinking that you are accomplishing more. The reality is that you are more busy than you are productive. Being busy, switching from task to task, prevents you from making forward progress on any one task.

You must complete the most important task first and while doing so, nothing else should exist. There is an 80/20 rule that says, "80% of your results come from just 20% of your efforts." If you double your time on the most important producing activities and stop doing others, you will double your output and spend 60% less time. Meaning, you can cut your work day and get twice as much accomplished.

Also, many people use free time to take on more commitments; often making them so tightly scheduled that it cascades to more projects than expected. You must learn to decline some opportunities. There is a limit to how much you can do. You can manage that limit and do things well, or you can ignore the limit and do a lousy job on everything. The choice is yours.

Chapter Checkpoint:

What can you do better to manage your time more wisely?

What will you do to make sure you are being productive instead of just being busy?

What will you do differently to make sure that you are working smarter?

Some ways to work smarter are to plan, organize, commit, and enjoy. Schedule your tasks throughout the days, weeks, and months. Specify time frames in which tasks should be completed, rather than setting deadlines which can be stressful. Make sure that you are committed and consistent in your efforts to ensure that your work gets completed. Turn your tasks into habits and remember, NO PROCRASTINATION OR EXCUSES!

Always get good sleep (7-8 hours), so that your body and mind function optimally. Get an early start and remember to devote your entire focus to the task at hand. Stay focused on one task at a time and do not allow unimportant details to consume your time.

If you really want to be productive, limit your visitors as well. Visits can mean doing lots of talking, catching up from past to current times, and burning up time. Be conscientious of your time spent watching television, playing games, browsing the internet, and viewing and chatting on social media sites. They can be the biggest drains on productivity.

You may find yourself in a place of needing to block out a certain amount of hours each day for focus time. This means, that you close yourself up in a room alone, forward the phone to voicemail or power it off, and work to build your rhythm. Having a certain time blocked out, will definitely help you get a few hours of solid work under your belt.

Lastly, take the time to reward yourself for goal attainment. Yes, getting work done is your primary focus, but work can be play. Enjoy what you are doing, even while you are working. Be happy while embracing your passions, and working smarter and you will enjoy the benefit of sitting at the dinner table with your family/children.

4 *How Can You Benefit Others?*

There is a growing trend in our society where people are becoming less compassionate for one another. In being so, they are separated one from another. So often, there seems to be a tendency of individuals focusing more on themselves, to the exclusion of our fellow human beings.

Although it doesn't apply to everyone, selfishness can make helping a person (other than yourself) appear to be an inconvenience. Self-focus often prevents one from recognizing the advantages of helping or benefiting others.

Not only can acts of kindness toward others be passed on and multiplied, it can slowly but surely help make the world a better place as well. In many cases, people are looking and hoping to make connections with kind and caring people to take advantages of positive opportunities. Positive opportunities can possibly help improve the lifestyle of an individual. When people see positive changes in their lives, it gives them a sense of hope for the future, and a positive self-image. Often, that makes them less likely to engage in crime. The less crime, the better the world. Wouldn't you feel great if you were able to make a difference in the world?

Ways to benefit others:

Be friendly- Being friendly to others can often make a person's day a little better. Even something as small as a smile on your face can put warm feelings in a person's heart, and a smile on their face as well.

<u>Be compassionate</u>- Show concern for others when you notice their distress, with a willingness to help make it easier to endure or lessen.

<u>Show love</u>- Find ways to express your love to others; even strangers. A kind word or a small hug matters more than you will ever know.

Be a teacher- Teach someone something that they may not know. Take the time to teach a friend a new computer skill to prepare for a new job. Teach another business owner some new marketing strategies. Teach an elderly family member how to use e-mail. Teaching others, can go a long way.

Lend an ear- Listen when a person is feeling bothered by something. Some people feel the need to share things with a close source or someone who would not be biased to their situation. Having someone to talk to while you are facing difficulty can be a huge help.

Be a helper- Volunteer to help the sick, shut ins and elderly. Help a good friend prepare or update their resume. Help a family member with planning a wedding. Help a co-worker plan and complete a project. Help a student complete a very important assignment. Many are in need of help and are very appreciative for it.

Encourage others- help build confidence in others by acknowledging things that they do well. Support other people and inspire them to follow their dreams or the desires of their heart. Share positive words and messages with others on a daily basis. Words of encouragement can help people take action on making necessary life decisions. Just a quick word of encouragement to others on a consistent basis, shows others that you care about what's going on with them or how they are feeling. Saying something as small as, "Never give up" or "You can do it", may be just enough to encourage someone to move forward, to get to the next level in their life.

Be patient- Often, people understand or learn at a different pace from others. Understand that what may seem easy or common sense to you, may be a little more difficult for another person to grasp. Learn to be patient with others.

PATIENCE IS KEY!

Show appreciation- Giving thanks or praise to someone shows that you appreciate them. Acknowledging someone before a public audience can really make a person feel good about themselves. Also, giving others a thank you card with a personal note enclosed can make a person not only feel appreciated, but valued as well.

Help someone take action- If you know someone that desires to do something but just doesn't know how or where to start at, help them. Show them what it takes to begin by helping them create an action plan, and help get them motivated to take immediate action.

Chapter Checkpoint:

How do you initially respond to people who are in need?

What have you done over the past 30 days to help someone else?

How have you benefited from the help of others?

After reading the first portion of this chapter, how do you think that you can benefit others?

Write down the names of 3 people that you think that you can help or benefit and why?

Contact the 3 people TODAY, and offer your help!

One of the most important ways to benefit others is to help them develop professionally. Keep in mind that skills enhancement can affect a person's future at a multitude of levels. Therefore, it's critical that a person keep up with training and skill enhancing opportunities.

People are often seeking a promotion or to land their dream job, but don't possess the skills required and have no clue of how to obtain them. You can easily add value to a person's life by helping them find professional networks and mentors. With your help, one can obtain advice, feedback, and information about advancements and other professional opportunities.

If you know a person who is unemployed or looking for new opportunities, offer to partner with them. Help them to set professional development goals and create a plan to meet those goals. Example: Set up time frames. Also, if you are the person who's seeking help, partnering and working with others is still a great idea. By working with other people outside of your usual comfort zone, you are going to find new ways to communicate, collaborate, and solve problems. The more ideas, the better the chance you have at finding numerous opportunities.

The act of helping people is a reward, not a penalty! You have a chance to build close relationships and become a part of a wider network that can end up shaping your own career in unexpected ways. Helping people can create great connections, and possibly help you develop into a future boss or business owner.

Chapter Checkpoint:

What do you think will be your biggest personal benefit to helping others?

What type of influence did this chapter have on your thoughts of benefiting or helping others?

What will you do today (for sure) to help someone else?

Do not neglect working with others, but learn to work with others. Commit your time to cultivate critical-thinking and problem-solving abilities, and foster great communication skills. It's a great way to improve your skills and possibly work with people who have already achieved goals similar to your own.

We currently live in a fast paced world, so you must be savvy and think big. Work with others so that they not only grow, but you do as well. Joining people who desire to further their skills can open a wide range of promotion possibilities and higher earning potential for each of you.

5 _How To Attract The Right People_

In chapter 2, I advised you to evaluate your circle of influence. In this chapter, I would like to extend on that by sharing with you how to attract the right people into your life.

Most people desire to be associated or connected with good people. In order to do so, you must model being the same type of person that you are interested in attracting. It's very important that you know who you are and what you want.

Chapter Checkpoint:

Who are you?

What do you want?

What is your purpose in life?

What qualities or values are you searching for in others?

Do you possess the same qualities or values? If not, why not?

When attracting people, most people look to attract others who have similar characteristics and desires. For example: If you are a person who is focused on being successful, it would be a great idea for you to start connecting with people who are motivated to achieve something in their life. To do so, you must focus on having a lot of confidence in your own abilities, so that you are attracting "above average people."

You may be asking, "What would be wrong with attracting below average people?" I wouldn't say that there is personally anything wrong with the individual, but I would say that they may not possess the qualities that you are looking for. They may not possess the qualities to reach the levels of success that you are interested in reaching, if they are beneath average. Think about being a student in high school. Who do you think would have a better chance to earn a full scholarship to the college of their choice? The student who is below average (D+) or the student who is above average (B+)? The student who is considered to be below average, may NOT have an option of being accepted to any college at all. Therefore, their options are limited.

Whatever it is that you desire to be, it would be wise to "think and act as if you already are." Get out and start meeting people who work in creative industries. Most of those people are making a living out of their passions. If they can do it, YOU CAN DO IT as well. Keep in mind that people in our lives are often a mirror for what we feel in ourselves. That's why it's important to connect with people who are already making it happen by living their dreams.

Think of a friend or colleague that you really like. There is something about them that sets them apart from others, and they are like a magnet to people. If you could describe what you like most about them in three words, what would they be?

Now, be really honest with yourself. Do you have these three qualities as well? Often what we like in others is what we like about ourselves. That is because we attract people who are like ourselves. Have you ever met a person for the very first time ever, but felt like you knew them forever? Of course you have. The reason is because you have found similarities in the two of you, and energetically it feels so right.

Attracting the right type of people reinforces the great qualities you possess within yourself. It keeps you motivated to keep pressing forward to continue to increase your circle of influence; with attracting more of the same type of individuals. On the other hand, if you are attracting people who are negative with poor qualities ask yourself, what are the three things that you dislike most about them? Ask yourself, do you possess any of those same negative qualities? Answer honestly. If you have answered yes to any of the three, work to get rid of them IMMEDIATELY!

Chapter Checkpoint:

What negative qualities do you need to get rid of and why?

What positive qualities do you need to possess and why?

What are some of the primary qualities that your immediate circle of influence possess (whether they are good or bad)?

    Honestly, what kind of relationships are you really attracting? There are usually patterns to your relationships, whether they are good or bad. There are often common personality traits. When you build relationships, think about who the person reminds you of and why. Is that good or bad? Make a decision to attract strong, sharp, wonderful, inspiring, and supportive people. The best way to do that is to model or be a person with all of those characteristics, and expect that to come back to you in return.

If you are an employee, ask yourself "Am I easy to work with?" "Do I go to work with a smile on my face, or do I have a monster mug?" "Am I friendly and polite, or mean and grumpy?" Make your intentions to be full of joy and compassion towards others. If you are a boss, ask yourself "Am I understanding and fun to work for?" Being understanding and fun will inspire employees to go above and beyond, and to be more productive. Or, "Am I intimidating, controlling, and bossy?" Behaving in that manner will bring down the morale of the employee/s and possibly discourage them from coming to work at all, which could result in a high employee turnover rate. Is your employee turnover rate high? If so, why? Make your intentions to be a kind and caring boss.

If you are a business owner, ask yourself what type of clients are you attracting. Are your clients a pleasure to work with? Or, do you get a headache just thinking of them. Believe in your skills 100%, and that you deserve to earn whatever amount of money from your profession that you request. Set the expectation that you expect to be paid on time, for clients to show up on time, and for clients to respect your time, just as you will respect theirs. Your clients are just reflecting your state of mind back at you. Choose to work with honest and respectful clients, and you will.

Lastly, are you happy within? Or, do you murmur and complain about everything that doesn't appear to go your way? Be happy, so that you can attract happy people who seem to have good things happening in their life on a regular basis. Attract people who can inspire you and expect the same. Have confidence and believe in yourself and believe that you will attract awesome people, because that will certainly be a reflection of how you feel about yourself.

Congratulations! You have just completed the first half of "Think Up And Go Up!"….If you are still reading, I KNOW THIS BOOK IS FOR YOU!

Please take a few moments to reflect on some of the things that you were experiencing while reading. The next half of this book only gets better!

6 *Become An Expert*

Do you really want to become an expert at what you do? Becoming an expert is possible but not always easy. It often takes hard work, focus, and dedication. The problem is that many people lack what it takes. Some often wonder what are the short cuts and fastest ways to become an expert. While I do agree that some people gain expert-level skills and knowledge on multiple subjects quickly; I don't agree that there are any ways around focusing, working hard, and dedicating time.

To become an expert, you must have expertise and experience. Meaning, that you must find a balance between learning something and doing it. You cannot be an expert at something that you have never done. You cannot be an expert at something without learning the best practices and principles. You must LEARN AND DO IT!

Often experts find additional help to ensure that they have maximum performance. They understand that finding additional help can uncover opportunities for improvement, along with getting them to the "expert-level" much quicker than working alone. They usually have successful friends, professional coaches, and/or mentors to hold them accountable, and help them improve in areas where they may be weak.

Experts are willing to learn their mistakes. Top performance universally, requires extensive practice. Therefore, mistakes are inevitable. Mistakes are a part of the learning process. Most experts are not so talented but rather exceptionally skilled due to having the right training. Extensive and consistent practice help people to steadily improve their performance.

If you desire to be an expert, you must be continually willing to challenge yourself to accomplish things at a slightly higher level, even if it's broken down into small steps. Self-feedback is usually not the best feedback because you often miss opportunities, causing it to be inaccurate. You may not like feedback because it may not always be what you would like to hear, but it's necessary and important. You need someone to help push you to perform slightly better than you normally would. It also helps to have someone guide your learning. Your coach/mentor would usually be the best person to provide you with more accurate feed back.

Chapter Checkpoint:

Why do you want to become an expert?

What do you need to do to become an expert?

What steps are you already taking to become an expert?

What expertise or experience do you have in your area of interest?

How has this chapter helped you so far?

    Becoming an expert is a smart idea for more reasons than one. Focusing on becoming an expert will help you to understand your business much better. The better you understand your business, the better your content or product will be to people who have never read or used it before. If you are an expert, people care about what you think and what you know.

    Experts have an easier time understanding exactly what they need than the average professional, because they know their market so well. Experts can often predict changes to their market and prepare for a shift.

When people know that you are an expert at something, you attract more attention than an ordinary person because they think you are smart and motivated. They are more likely to believe your opinion when you know more. Therefore, they want to connect with you, support you, and purchase your products.

Being an expert can afford you numerous opportunities to be in the spotlight. You will find yourself being asked for interviews by the media and other experts. They desire to meet and interview experts who are well informed on their topic. Being well informed makes you an attractive person. And other important people are drawn to you. They may also be interested in a collaboration with you. Being given an opportunity to be in the media can open numerous windows of opportunities.

When you earn a great deal of respect, you have a great chance of growing a social media following, without doing a great deal of work.

People start looking and researching to find you because they have heard about you. They want to connect with you and share comments on your posts.

Learn your topic and teach it better than any other experts. Stay relevant by keeping your products out there and consistently adding to them. The more you have to offer, the better. The better your topic, the more shares, likes, and tweets you get in social media which allows your message to move further and further each and every day.

Besides, experts make more money because people don't mind paying more for your products or services, if you are known to be the best!

Chapter Checkpoint:

What is your topic?

How well do you know your topic?

Have you ever been interviewed by the media and other experts? If so, why?

Why is your topic any better than another person who has a similar topic?

What will you do to be more informed about your topic?

7 *Challenge Yourself*

Challenging ourselves is essential to improving as individuals and enhancing the quality of our lives. Challenge helps to grow your skills and knowledge; along with growing your belief that you can achieve something that you always wondered if you could. Challenge equals change. When we stretch our capabilities beyond our comfort zone, WE CHANGE! You never know how many new things you can learn until you are determined enough to try hard.

It is very important that you challenge yourself mentally, emotionally, and physically in order to see positive changes in your life. Begin to stretch yourself mentally by thinking and creating different exercises each day. Example: Make a list of ten reasons to move away from your comfort zone. Doing activities like that on a daily basis will help stretch your mind a little more each day. Stretch yourself emotionally by acknowledging your fears and taking small steps that will help you get over them. Example: If you desire to be an artist but you are afraid of that blank piece of paper that sits in front of you, JUST MAKE A MARK

ON IT anywhere. Just as long as the paper is no longer blank, you have STARTED somewhere. Put your emotions into your work, bring your personality to the table, and allow your passion to show. Stretch yourself physically. Start being active on a daily basis. Of course exercise would be the best way to be active. Example: If you can't get yourself into jogging several miles a day, lifting weights, or spending time on the treadmill; maybe you can walk your dog in the mornings, walk around the mall for an hour, or do housework. You will be far ahead of the crowd if you consistently challenge your personal beliefs, as well as what you know.

Chapter Checkpoint:

What have you challenged yourself to do within the past week?

What have you accomplished by challenging yourself?

What was one of your most difficult challenges?

What are some things that you are going to start doing to challenge yourself more?

If you want to make the most out of what you would like to accomplish, you must CHALLENGE

YOURSELF! Although you may feel more safe sticking to what you know, it never forces you to rise above the every day normal. You will NEVER fulfill even a small fraction of your potential by "playing it safe" and remaining in your comfort zone. That's because your comfort zone doesn't offer the resistance that strengthens the muscles you didn't even know you had. You must do something that stretches you beyond the feelings of safety, that allows you a chance to engage in a way that being comfortable doesn't.

If you have been siting in neutral, MOVE forward, so you can begin to thrive in a challenge. Start off slow and gradually pick up your speed. Although it may feel a little shaky, it will begin to feel doable. The more you keep moving, the more confidence you will have in doing it. You will soon realize that you challenged yourself and YOU SUCCEEDED! Once you have successfully completed that, challenge yourself to turn your attention to accomplishing something else.

Be determined not to place limitations on expanding your mind. You cannot grow personally or professionally if your mind is in a complacent and inactive state. You must seek and attain awareness, knowledge, and education. The more you know, the more you will begin to realize how little you actually understand. IT'S TIME TO REMOVE THE LIMITATIONS!

If you want more in life you must challenge yourself. Otherwise, you are not likely to get it. If you want to be healthy, challenge yourself to exercise and eat better. If you want to be wealthy, challenge yourself to make more, save more, and have more money. Accomplishing goals always start with positioning yourself to accomplish them.

If you are consistently making an effort to do something that may not be so easy but rewarding, your life will definitely become more fulfilling. This is because you will begin to meet new people, learn new things, have more fun, and may even be offered new opportunities that lead to a more fruitful career.

Seek inspiration by challenging yourself to find ways to become inspired. Whether you want to be a cook or a doctor, you are in need of being creative. Seeking inspiration is a never ending quest that requires real diligence. Being creative will definitely set you apart from others and can contribute to your success. When one reaches success, they usually find happiness and peace. Why not have more happiness and peace in your life? IT'S TIME TO UNBLOCK YOUR CREATIVITY!

Chapter Checkpoint:

How has this chapter inspired you?

In what ways do you think that challenging yourself can help you?

What are some of the limitations that you have placed on yourself?

What will you do to be more creative?

8 *Take Action*

How many times have you told yourself that you were going to do something but never did? How many times have you told yourself that you were going to take advantage of a great opportunity and you waited and went back and attempted to, but the opportunity was GONE? In many cases, you have done those things because you are complacent (not content) where you are. Therefore, you procrastinated and missed it. You must find a way to start moving with an optimistic attitude of change in mind.

There are so many people/professionals who feel like they've earned degrees, had major accomplishments, and have done ENOUGH in life to sustain their success. The truth is that they have become complacent in life and don't want to commit to change or add any new skills to their current skills. While great communication and leadership skills will always be necessary, they have become very basic today. Technological skills are consistently changing and you must be able to adapt, because it's a part of everyday life.

Of course you should keep what works, but you must focus on improving or making it better as well. This is the 21st century, and what you did to sustain in the 20th century may no longer work. You may know something that worked in the past but it makes sense to learn something that is much more improved. You must be creative and increase, sharpen, and change your skills at all times; in order to keep up with what works TODAY. Otherwise, you may find yourself as being less valuable in your own market. You may even end up without a job or business. TAKE ACTION to keep growing, and you will always be up-to-date and needed by someone.

Chapter Checkpoint:

What is one major thing that you need to take action on but have not?

What is stopping you from taking action?

What will you do going forward to prevent those things from stopping you to take action?

What new skills are you in need of?

What will you do to acquire the new skills?

Sometimes, you have to back away from things for a little while because you need a short mental or physical break. Keep in mind that if you stay away too long, you may not finish. Not completing something is worse than not starting at all. We know what we should be doing but we would rather do things that are much easier. For example: Watching television, listening to music, or spending time on social networks may be much easier than what we should be doing.

There is no perfect plan for taking action. There will be pain and difficulties, because you will make mistakes and face rejection. As long as you work on your plan, you can protect yourself. As long as you move away from procrastination, you will be fine. We often make jobs that are very easy, appear to be difficult because we keep postponing our TAKE ACTION date. The longer we postpone it, the further it gets away from being accomplished, which often leads to being unaccomplished. SIMPLIFY YOUR LIFE BY TAKING ACTION!

We are often told to "stop thinking and start doing." While this may be something you should be doing, to avoid making a mountain out of a molehill; it is equally important that you not overthink things. Although you want to start something with an end in mind, you must be careful. Overthinking things by looking too far in the future can make your goal seem impossible. When something seems impossible, "you shut down." Shift your focus back to what you can do or what is possible TODAY, at the present moment and start there. When you take your first step, each step thereafter will get a little easier to take, because you are no longer resistant. Even big dreams are created one baby step at a time.

Start with the hardest task first. Once you get the hard things out of the way, you will feel much better about yourself. You will notice that your confidence is being built up and tasks will become much easier to accomplish. Taking actions in what's going to build you up to what you desire to be. What you do on a regular basis will determine who you are. If you are lazy and doing nothing, you will be a procrastinator. If you are motivated and determined, you will take action.

Although positive affirmations alone won't get you where you want to be, it's good to speak and write them regularly. This can help condition your mind into a habit of positive thought patterns. You want taking action to be a natural and easy part of your life, so it's important to think and speak positive. Positive affirmations often begin with words like, I will, I can, or I am. Use this chapter to help develop parts of your mind that you have been struggling to change. If you do, you will find yourself becoming naturally proactive, and taking less effort to take action when you want to get things done.

Chapter Checkpoint:

How has this chapter benefited you?

After reading this chapter, how hard will it be for you to begin to take action?

What is your plan of action?

How will you respond to making mistakes while taking action?

How are you going to motivate yourself into taking action?

Are your actions supporting your business vision? If not, why not?

You have now been called to TAKE ACTION!

9 Be Determined To Win

Are you consistently taking action, even when you feel like sitting still? Or, are you sitting around with a bunch of written words on a paper, claiming to have a plan? Perhaps you have a dream and although you have been working long and hard to achieve it, you still can't seem to get there. Sometimes, you feel like relinquishing yourself to the enemy called "failure" but you know that your circumstances won't allow you to. It has been said that, "when you can't change your circumstances, you are challenged to change yourself."

Even when you feel 100% powerless, you have to remain hopeful and keep the faith to overcome those feelings of fear or failure. That's called DETERMINATION. Be determined to succeed by focusing your attention on the direction you would like to go, instead of on the direction you have been. Your past has no bearing on your future, but your present does. You must manage to persevere.

If you lack determination, you CAN'T win. The difference between a winner and a loser is

DETERMINATION! You may not be able to accomplish everything in one day but if you are determined, you will definitely make it happen. Have confidence in yourself and make your dreams your priority, because just having a roadmap (alone) to your dream will not be enough. You must be determined to get the best and give the best to the world in order to win.

Determination is the key to turning your idea into an achievement. It requires that you remove all limitations, and overcome the barriers that come before you. In order to do so, you must stay extremely focused. Think about when, how, and where you do your best work. These are usually the places and times at which you are more motivated and inspired to get your work done.

You are a unique individual. You know your strengths and weakness better than anyone else. Invest your time in the things that you want by taking on more tasks that are directly associated with what you would like to earn, gain, or achieve. Reduce tasks that don't align with your goals.

Chapter Checkpoint:

What was something you were determined to accomplish (good or bad) and did? How?

How determined are you to fulfill your passion?

How many times have you quit and why?

Where do you feel more productive at and why?

Determination also requires preparation. You must be prepared to always think independently.

Don't allow people to think for you. You must stick to what you believe, because there will be people who tell you that you need to slow down and take it easy. They will tell you that you are overworking yourself by doing way too much. Honestly, they are most likely the people who are doing TOO LITTLE because they fail to realize that you can soar as high as you want to; IF YOU WANT TO.

You have to work much harder than the average person, to make sure that you are one of the first to be given great opportunities as they become available. You will not be overlooked if you are capable and determined. Be prepared to share your success stories, so that you stand out among others. Don't be afraid to live by your own values. Don't' have any doubts or allow anyone to push you in the opposite direction of your vision.

You will certainly face obstacles; just as every other successful person has, but be positive at all times. Be optimistic about your future and know exactly what you are striving for. When you are clear with what you want to accomplish, you are more focused. The more focused you are, the more you grow. The more you grow, the more fulfilled you are. Keep pressing to build yourself up and stay on the correct path to your destiny. Stay fueled up to keep your engine running toward your dreams. KEEP MOVING FORWARD!

Regardless of your setbacks, staying on course and having a positive attitude leads you to one option. That option is SUCCESS. Just keep putting one foot in front of the other and visualize the success you're working to attain because it's definitely within your reach.

Chapter Checkpoint:

What obstacles or setbacks have you faced?

What are you striving for and why?

What type of attitude do you have?

What additional opportunities have determination afforded you?

Don't fight the impulse of making your dream a reality!

10 *From Motivation To Elevation*

Being motivated is always great. The question is, when your song and dance is over what do you do next? Another words, how long do you feel motivation after the motivational message was given? So often, people hear great messages which really inspire and motivate them to get moving. After a few days or a few weeks (at most), the feeling is gone and they are back where they started; in a slump or just not feeling it.

One of the most important elements to keeping you excited, determined, committed, and interested in taking action to completing a task is "self motivation." You must find ways to be self motivated. When an individual is self motivated, the body and mind are able to subconsciously condition themselves to satisfy the requirements of the individual to successfully accomplish their goals.

Sometimes you have to think and come up with ideas that will help motivate you. For example: Giving yourself a small reward as you accomplish a goal can help. Rewards are usually enjoyable and a great way to help you stay motivated.

Reminders to yourself can also help. Constant reminders about how much more fulfilling you life can be if you accomplish your goals, will make you want to get moving.

Although you may not always find joy in self motivation, finding something that brings on positive feelings can help motivate you as well. Keep in mind that if you are excited or have a positive feeling about something, that could be the inspiration needed to carry your mindset to take action and get something accomplished. If you are excited, there will be very little need for you to be pushed to do something.

Be sure to always keep a positive mindset. Be optimistic and you will find that it's much easier for you to accomplish whatever you wish. Continuously look for positive elements; even in negative situations. People who focus on being positive, regardless of the situation, are much easier to stay motivated.

Listening to inspirational or motivational messages are a great way to motivate yourself. People who advocate a constant positive mindset, can often impart invaluable information; which can help you move to a greater level. So let's not forget, that there are plenty of merits in ensuring that you have a positive mindset.

Chapter Checkpoint:

What has been able to keep you motivated for long periods of time?

What will you do to keep yourself motivated?

How is your mindset when you are faced with difficulty?

What type of motivational messages do you listen to? How often?

As you practice having a positive mindset, how will you help others do the same?

Having a positive mindset affords you an opportunity to impart as many great values as possible, into others who want to have a positive outlook on life as well. This mindset will certainly help you stay motivated, and when you are motivated, goals are more visible. They appear to be firmly imprinted in the mind's eye because your excitement level is high.

Having a love or a passion for what you do will keep you motivated. When you really like something, you focus more on the goal and less on what it takes to get there. If you are motivated, you will be dedicated. If you are dedicated, you will be elevated to great levels of success, which leads to much personal gratification.

Your motivation and dedication is now helping you to move forward or advance. Being motivated helps you to venture into getting accustomed to a routine, and being focused on accomplishing the goals set before you; within an allotted time frame. Staying motivated will keep your mind active and creative. When you are active and creative, you excel.

You gain leverage over your competitors because your true key differential is "YOURSELF." The more active and creative you are, the more attractive you are to people; which gives you an advantage over another competitor. You are elevated much faster than the ordinary person in your market.

Continue to sharpen your thinking. Sharpening your thinking will help you maintain your competitive edge. The sharper you are, the more doors there will be to open; and enable your work to be of a higher quality than others in your industry. Continue with challenges that strengthen your competitive advantage and will keep you soaring far beyond. In doing so, you will begin to see how your "MOTIVATION took you to ELEVATION."

Chapter Checkpoint:

How visible are your goals?

How creative are you?

What will you do to sharpen your thinking?

Why would people be more attracted to you than your competitors?

What did you learn from this chapter?

Congratulations! You have just completed the second half of "Think Up And Go Up!"

I hope that this book was enjoyable and helpful. Please take a few moments to reflect on some of the things that you were experiencing while reading.

Positive Thinking Quotes

"A pessimist sees the difficulty in every opportunity; an optimist sees the opportunity in every difficulty."....***Winston Churchill***

"The positive thinker sees the invisible, feels the intangible, and achieves the impossible."....***Unknown***

"Anyone who has never made a mistake has never tried anything new."....***Albert Einstein***

"Success is not final, failure is not fatal: it is the courage to continue that counts."....***Winston Churchill***

"Once you replace negative thoughts with positive ones, you'll start having positive results."....***Willie Nelson***

"A positive attitude may not solve all your problems, but it will annoy enough people to make it worth the effort."….**Herm Albright**

"There is little difference in people, but that little difference makes a big difference. The little difference is attitude. The big difference is whether it is positive or negative."….**W. Clement Stone**

Challenge Quotes

"Life's challenges are not supposed to paralyze you, they're supposed to help you discover who you are."....***Bernice Johnson Reagon***

"Accept the challenges so that you may feel the exhilaration of victory."....***General George S. Patton***

"Don't be afraid to fail. Don't waste energy trying to cover up failure. Learn from your failures and go on to the next challenge. It's OK to fail. If you're not failing, you're not growing."....***Unknown***

"Opportunities to find deeper powers within ourselves come when life seems most challenging."....***Joseph Campbell***

"Competing at the highest level is the greatest test of one's character."….***Russell Mark***

"Give yourself an even greater challenge than the one you are trying to master and you will develop the powers necessary to overcome the original difficulty."….***William Bennett***

Determination Quotes

"Determination and perseverance move the world; thinking that others will do it for you is a sure way to fail."…. **Marva Collins**

"The question isn't who is going to let me; it's who is going to stop me."…. **Ayn Rand**

Success is a ladder you cannot climb with your hands in your pockets."…. **American Proverb**

"The best way out is always through."…. **Robert Frost**

"Strength is a matter of the made-up mind."…. **John Beecher**

The difference between a successful person and others is not a lack of strength, not a lack of knowledge, but rather a lack of will."…. **Vincent T. Lombardi**

"Real leaders are ordinary people with extraordinary determination. " **Unknown Author**

Motivational Quotes

"Accept responsibility for your life. Know that it is you who will get you where you want to go, no one else."…. **Les Brown**

"In order to succeed, your desire for success should be greater than your fear of failure."…. **Bill Cosby**

Don't be afraid to stand for what you believe in, even if that means standing alone"….**Unknown**

"Life is like photography. You need the negatives to develop."….**Unknown**

"Build your own dreams, or someone else will hire you to build theirs."….**Farrah Gray**

"The only thing that stands between you and your dream is the will to try and the belief that it is actually possible."….***Joel Brown***

"Self confidence is the most attractive quality a person can have. How can anyone see how awesome you are if you can't see it yourself?"….***Unknown***

"Forget all the reasons it won't work and believe the one reason that it will."…. ***Unknown***

"Three things you cannot recover in life: the WORD after it's said, the MOMENT after it's missed and the TIME after it's gone. Be Careful!"….***Unknown***

Contact The Author

If you would like to write in reference to this book, request more copies, or contact the author, please feel free to do so at:

Andrea Freeman

P.O. Box 18151

Baltimore, MD 21220

info@authorandreafreeman.com

www.authorandreafreeman.com

(443)478-8500

Also available for purchase:

"No Barriers, No Limits!"….Andrea Freeman

Author websites:

www.classyaccessories.net

www.classy5.org

www.authorandreafreeman.com

www.ingramcontent.com/pod-product-compliance
Lightning Source LLC
LaVergne TN
LVHW021404080426
835508LV00020B/2458